CW00384054

The SENDCO

Book 1 a – The SENDCO Solutions Support Series

APRIL 1, 2018

www.sendcosolutions.co.uk

Abigail Hawkins

Copyright © 2018 Abigail Hawkins

All rights reserved.

ISBN-13: 9781980782612

The SENDCO

Reproduction rights: All reproduction rights are reserved, and no part of the book may be reproduced or transmitted in any form or by any means, electronically or mechanically, including photocopying, scanning or any other information storage or retrieval system, without prior written permission from the Publisher.

Website contents: The proforma provided on the website are for the use of the purchaser within his/her educational establishment. The files cannot be shared outside the establishment, in forums, copied or transmitted electronically by any means.

This series of booklets is written to support SENDCOs.

The information is current as of March 1st 2018.

A couple of notes:

SENDCO, SENCO, INCO, ALNCO, Vulnerable Groups Co-ordinator, LD Co-Ordinator, Inclusion Manager, SEN Coordinator (legal), etc. => **SENDCO/SENCO** (sorry if you use a different title.)

Student, Pupil, Child, Young Person, CYP, etc. => **Pupil**

TA, Teaching Assistant, LSA, Learning Support Assistant, LA, Learning Assistant, SNA, Special Needs Assistant, LM, Learning Mentor, Mentor, Support Assistant, etc. => **TA**

SLT, Senior Leadership Team, SMT, Senior Management Team, Higher Leadership, etc. => **SLT**

Headteacher, HT, Principal, Executive Principal, etc. => **Headteacher**

School, college, nursery, establishment, academy, etc. => **School**

Contents

Introduction

 I once started a CPD session on differentiation with a slide showing Granny how to suck eggs.

This must be one of the most difficult chapters I had to write in this series. Why? Because it really does feel like teaching Granny to suck eggs!

You have your job role because you already know what a SENDCO is and what your job is supposed to be. It should also be detailed in your job description.

If you are expecting to read a chapter with the History of Education, I'm sorry to disappoint. I will make reference to relevant sections but I'm not going to go into detail about the 1944 Education Act, the 1834 Poor Act or Warnock's report of 1978. If you do need this information, Google it! (or have a look at chapter 1 in Rita Cheminais' Handbook for SENCOs for a summary of changes to SEN since 1981.)

You and Your Role

If you had the role before 2014 then there is a vague possibility you may not be aware that your role significantly changed with the Children and Families Act and the subsequent new SEND Code of Practice that followed in January 2015. Whilst I, and all other authors frequently make reference to the SEND Code of Practice (2015) the underlying legislation lies within the Children and Families Act 2014[1]. This can be quite an important and useful piece of information, since there are elements of the Code of Practice open to interpretation whereas the legislation is quite clear.

The part about your role appears in Part 3 section 67 of the legislation:

> **SEN co-ordinators**
> (1)This section imposes duties on the appropriate authorities of the following schools in England—
> (a)mainstream schools;
> (b)maintained nursery schools.
> (2)The appropriate authority must designate a member of staff at the school (to be known as the "SEN co-ordinator") as having responsibility for co-ordinating the provision for pupils with special educational needs
> (3)Regulations may—
> (a)require appropriate authorities which are subject to the duty imposed by subsection (2) to ensure that SEN co-ordinators have prescribed qualifications or prescribed experience (or both);
> (b)confer other functions relating to SEN co-ordinators on appropriate authorities which are subject to the duty imposed by subsection (2).
> (4)The "appropriate authority" for a school is—
> (a)in the case of a maintained school or maintained nursery school, the governing body;
> (b)in the case of an Academy, the proprietor.

So basically, your school must employ a SENDCO (called a SEN co-ordinator in law) and ensure you have

---

[1] Children and Families Act, 2014. *https://www.legislation.gov.uk/ukpga/2014/6/pdfs/ukpga_20140006_en.pdf*

appropriate qualifications/experience. The Children and Families Act (2014) was an adaptation to the Education Act (1996). It is worth noting that different law exists in Wales and Northern Ireland, with Wales currently revising its SEN legislation, hence I write with regard to English law. I'm sure in due course I'll write additional versions of this book to reflect the differences.

There were a couple of laws just before the 2014 changes, that clarify what happens next in the Code of Practice. In 2008 the Education Regulations (Special Educational Needs Coordinators, England) stated that the SENCO had to be a qualified teacher and the governing body was to monitor the effectiveness of the SENCO. At the same time the role was clarified and specified. This was amended in 2009 to require governing bodies to ensure any new SENCO should undertake training on a nationally approved scheme leading to the National Award for Special Educational Needs Coordination within three years of taking up the post.

The Code of Practice translates the law into day-to-day operations.

I am going to put in black and white what the Code of Practice says your role is. Why? Because sometimes we forget and either let someone convince us it says something different, or we have not been allowed to do a particular element for so long we have forgotten it was actually a key element! (And you might like to check your contract as well.) In some schools where the role is split, perhaps between an Inclusion Co-ordinator and SENDCO, it is useful to refer to the Code of Practice to ensure you are covering all the elements.

There are different elements to the Code of Practice with reference to your role.

Governor Responsiblities

> [2] 6.84 Governing bodies of maintained mainstream schools and the proprietors of mainstream academy schools (including free schools) **must** ensure that there is a qualified teacher designated as SENCO for the school.

The key thing here is *QUALIFIED TEACHER*. This was bought in with the 2008 changes to the Education Regulations[3] and is a legal requirement. The governors must hold the school to account on this. Prior to this there was an increasing number of TAs being delegated to the SENCO role but without the pay!

Qualifications

> 6.85 The SENCO **must** be a qualified teacher working at the school. A newly appointed SENCO **must** be a qualified teacher and, where they have not previously been the SENCO at that or any other relevant school for a total period of more than twelve months, they **must** achieve a National Award in Special Educational Needs Co-ordination within three years of appointment.
>
> 6.86 A National Award **must** be a postgraduate course accredited by a recognised higher education provider. The National College for Teaching and Leadership has worked with providers to develop a set of learning outcomes (see the References section under Chapter 6 for a link). When appointing staff or arranging for them to study for a National Award schools should satisfy themselves that the chosen course will meet these outcomes

---

[2] https://assets.publishing.service.gov.uk/government/uploads/system/uploads/attachment_data/file/398815/SEND_Code_of_Practice_January_2015.pdf

[3] https://www.legislation.gov.uk/uksi/2008/2945/pdfs/uksi_20082945_en.pdf

> and equip the SENCO to fulfil the duties outlined in this Code. Any selected course should be at least equivalent to 60 credits at postgraduate study.

So, if you're new to the role, you've got 3 years to secure yourself a Masters level qualification – the National Award in SEN Coordination (**NASENCO**). If, like me, you've held the role for at least 12 months, in another school or schools, then it is not a requirement.

Funding subsidies have now run out for this so schools must fund the qualification if appropriate. Costs are reasonable considering it is a Masters level qualification, however you must consider the time required to study. You must be employed in a school and have your Head Teacher's approval, regardless of who is footing the bill. Although you don't have to be in role, so this could be considered a professional development route for an aspiring SENDCO.

Online options, face to face training or a combination of both is available and most candidates complete the course in 9-18 months of starting, although you have 36 months from starting in role.

The training standards have changed little from the old Rainbow Guides (so called because of their highly distinctive covers) introduced in 1998 by the Teacher Training Agency: *National Standards for Special Educational Needs Coordinators*.

Role

> 6.87 The SENCO has an important role to play with the headteacher and governing body, in determining the strategic development of SEN policy and provision in the school. They will be most effective in that role if they are part of the school leadership team.

6.88 The SENCO has day-to-day responsibility for the operation of SEN policy and co-ordination of specific provision made to support individual pupils with SEN, including those who have EHC plans.

6.89 The SENCO provides professional guidance to colleagues and will work closely with staff, parents and other agencies. The SENCO should be aware of the provision in the Local Offer and be able to work with professionals providing a support role to families to ensure that pupils with SEN receive appropriate support and high-quality teaching.

OK, so you need to write a *POLICY*, decide what the school needs to do to meet its SEN obligations, co-ordinate a program of interventions (lessons) both on a strategic (overview) and also on an individual (pupil) level, work with *EVERYONE* and be able to find your way around your Local Authorities website to locate their *OFFER* and what they are expecting you as a school to deliver. As many local authorities do not have websites that are easily navigated you may well be the first port of call for desperate families who need signposting to the correct support.

This section is a little more woolly on whether you should, or should not, be a member of the school leadership team. There is no doubt that the role requires you to take leadership of the school and its staff, however in a large school you may find that you are not a part of the senior leadership team but of so-called middle leadership (the equivalent of heads of department or faculties) with a 'champion' who brings up SEN related issued at senior leadership meetings. It is important that the person representing you has a clear understanding of your role and the challenges you face to represent you coherently at the meetings, otherwise they will come back with some unrealistic expectations for you to navigate or not represent your needs adequately in a meeting.

Responsibilities

6.90 The key responsibilities of the SENCO may include:

• overseeing the day-to-day operation of the school's SEN policy

• co-ordinating provision for children with SEN

• liaising with the relevant Designated Teacher where a looked after pupil has SEN

• advising on the graduated approach to providing SEN support

• advising on the deployment of the school's delegated budget and other resources to meet pupils' needs effectively

• liaising with parents of pupils with SEN

• liaising with early years providers, other schools, educational psychologists, health and social care professionals, and independent or voluntary bodies

• being a key point of contact with external agencies, especially the local authority and its support services

• liaising with potential next providers of education to ensure a pupil and their parents are informed about options and a smooth transition is planned

• working with the headteacher and school governors to ensure that the school meets its responsibilities under the Equality Act (2010) with regard to reasonable adjustments and access arrangements

• ensuring that the school keeps the records of all pupils with SEN up to date

The key words here are **POLICY**, **PROVISION**, **CO-ORDINATE**, **LIAISE** and **ADVISE**. In addition to these roles you need to keep your **RECORDS** up to date and make sure the school is compliant with not just the SEND Code of Practice which is a legal document but also the **EQUALITY ACT**. You will find yourself the main named contact in a lot of people's diaries!

Just when you thought it was getting complicated with reference to law in the Children and Families Act, 2014, we now have reference to another law, the Equality Act

(2010)[4] which is under our remit to contend with. This is not the only law you need to be aware of since the Disability Discrimination Act (1995[5], 2005)[6] falls firmly under your responsibilities too, even though it is no longer explicitly mentioned. Somewhere in school you probably have an Accessibility Plan, don't be surprised if you are asked to update this (or at least contribute significant sections.)

School Responsibilities

6.91 The school should ensure that the SENCO has sufficient time and resources to carry out these functions. This should include providing the SENCO with sufficient administrative support and time away from teaching to enable them to fulfil their responsibilities in a similar way to other important strategic roles within a school.

6.92 It may be appropriate for a number of smaller primary schools to share a SENCO employed to work across the individual schools, where they meet the other requirements set out in this chapter of the Code. Schools can consider this arrangement where it secures sufficient time away from teaching and sufficient administrative support to enable the SENCO to fulfil the role effectively for the total registered pupil population across all of the schools involved.

6.93 Where such a shared approach is taken the SENCO should not normally have a significant class teaching commitment. Such a shared SENCO role should not be carried out by a headteacher at one of the schools.

6.94 Schools should review the effectiveness of such a shared SENCO role regularly and should not persist with it where there is evidence of a negative impact on the quality of SEN provision, or the progress of pupils with SEN.

Four bullet points to say one thing; you need *TIME* and *RESOURCES* to do your role effectively. Sadly, the Code

---

[4] Equality Act, 2010. https://www.legislation.gov.uk/ukpga/2010/15/pdfs/ukpga_20100015_en.pdf

[5] Disability Discrimination Act, 1995.
https://www.legislation.gov.uk/ukpga/1995/50/pdfs/ukpga_19950050_en.pdf

[6] Disability Discrimination Act, 2005.
https://www.legislation.gov.uk/ukpga/2005/13/pdfs/ukpga_20050013_en.pdf

of Practice doesn't go far enough and suggest a minimum amount of time! It should be noted that this is time that is additional to any PPA time you are given.

It also suggests that the role of SENDCO can be shared amongst several smaller schools provided this is not detrimental to the provision and progress within those schools.

Assistant SENDCOs are not mentioned, even in or for larger schools. This 'job title' has gained popularity over recent years with those seeking to further their career by undertaking the NASENCO award without taking on the full role until qualified, either as a succession to post within their own school or seen as a promotion to another school.

I recently asked a group of SENDCOs to tell me in a tweet what the job role of a SENDCO is.

(Twitter is definitely useful for getting people to be succinct.)

What is the role of a SENDCO (24.03.2018)

"Eternal optimist"

"SENDCOs need to ensure that every pupil receive what is required to help for achieving self, social, and academic goals."

"To recognise, plan for and implement effective teaching and learning for young people with SEND."

"Overseeing inclusion, coordinating support for SEND learners, leading staff and ensuring high expectations for all."

"Being a key and one of the most important partners in the understanding of your CYP, facilitating communication between all parties to ensure success"

Truth be told, when you took on the role of SENDCO you also took on the roles of:

A **SENDCO** is responsible for the day-to-day operation of the school's SEN policy. All mainstream schools must appoint a teacher to be their **SENDCO**. The **SENDCO** will co-ordinate additional support for pupils with SEN and liaise with their parents, teachers and other professionals who are involved with them.

Time Management

Well, that was straightforward! So, how much time do we have for doing everything listed above...and anything from the other roles we play in school? The very simple answer is, 'not enough!'

Let's for a second imagine we work in an 'average' school, with an 'average workload' and we are employed as a SENDCO and Class Teacher (but by some miracle someone else does all the other jobs.) For the purpose of making life simple we are going to have 25 teaching periods in a week and 10% PPA.

	An average Primary	An average Secondary
On role	279	946
K (12.2% primary 14.4% secondary)	34	136
E (1.3% primary 1.7% secondary)	4	16

Immediately we can see that it would be unreasonable to expect the Secondary SENDCO with 4 times the number of pupils to cater for to undertake their role in the same amount of time as a primary SENDCO.

Now, I've worked in all sectors (I'm ignoring FE for now) and I have to say that as a SENDCO it was much easier in a primary school. I had one member of teaching staff for each SEN pupil to deal with. Primary school teachers and their teaching assistants take far more responsibility for their learners and differentiation as part of whole class teaching means the majority of learners do not need direct SENDCO input. It does mean that as a SENDCO you have a greater role in ensuring your staff have the skills to identify and meet all needs. In our average school above I'm pretty sure that with the right processes behind me (and an understanding that the work load fluctuates throughout the year and I may need the odd spare hour when an urgent request comes in) I could cover the needs of the pupils on the 'SEN Register[7]' with a further 15% of time, although ideally 20% which would be one clear day a week just to concentrate on SEN related issues/meetings etc.

One of the things that senior leaders often fail to appreciate is that meetings have to fit around the availability of other professionals. Having my fixed SEN time on a Monday is no use if the professionals I need to meet with all work part time, Wednesday to Friday. By the way, Monday and Friday are the worst days, in my experience, for any PPA or delegated time, we lose too many of them to bank holidays and school special events; they are however, great for break duty! And on that note, if you do get a 'day off' timetable make sure it is not your duty day. Have a truly designated SEN day and if you want to observe playground interaction you can do it, but without having half your attention on the rest of the school at the same time.

If you need to negotiate minimum SEN time in a primary school then matching the percentage of time with the percentage of K pupils plus double the percentage of E pupils would be a good starting argument. (In my school here 12.2 + (2x1.3) = 14.8%)

In a secondary school, we have a whole different scenario to contend with. Not only do we usually have far more pupils to look after but you could be potentially dealing with 12 or more staff per pupil and a number of different teaching assistants, learning mentors etc.

---

[7] The SEN Register is not compulsory...but without a list of who has what need you will find it very difficult to keep track of your pupils.

In the secondary school example above, I'd ideally need at least 40% of the week to organize meetings, liaise with staff and professionals, meet parents, do observations etc. I'd be praying those 16 EHCPs are spaced evenly throughout the year (it's still one a fortnight)!

Secondary schools are generally more generous with PPA time, although it seems to be less protected and you do get drawn into cover. Again avoid duty on days where you have your SEN time either side, unless you like the "break".

Recall statement 6:91 from the Code of Practice

> 6.91 The school should ensure that the SENCO has sufficient time and resources to carry out these functions. This should include providing the SENCO with sufficient administrative support and time away from teaching to enable them to fulfil their responsibilities in a similar way to other important strategic roles within a school.

If you don't have the time or the support, you will not be able to fulfil your responsibilities. If you are fortunate enough to have a large team and the support of administrative staff or perhaps an assistant SENDCO then your school may well push back with an argument as to you need less time. This will depend on your own ability to delegate appropriately too.

I always feel the administrative element is seriously overlooked. There are many tasks we take on as teachers and just do without really considering if someone else is better placed to do them. Typing letters and mailing them is one of those tasks. It took me many years to realise that if I had a general format and then added one or two paragraphs of specific information I could save a lot of time...even more if I made sure someone in admin had my templates on file and just added my extra scribbles for me. A two or three sentence email is quicker to send myself, but photocopying a Connor's questionnaire, distributing it, collating, transferring the results to one sheet, typing a quick cover letter and mailing back to the paediatrician could be potentially quite time consuming and probably better delegated to someone within either the support team or admin.

Not Drinking Coffee

What should you be doing in the time allocated for your SENDCO duties?

The Code of Practice says... Don't make me write it again, it may well make the book longer but really is pointless! Look at sections 6.88-6.90 (pages 11-12).

The first thing it mentions is a **POLICY**, sometime **EVERYDAY** (just to check everything is OK and rearrange things for absent colleagues), a way to check on your **PROVISIONS** and a way to regularly check on your **PUPILS**.

Don't underestimate the amount of time it can take to write or review a policy. Whilst it is generally only undertaken once a year, they all seem to need doing at once. Once you've done your part it probably has to go through the senior leadership team and then needs to be ratified at a governors meeting. So, if you know your policy renewal date is July, start looking at the content before June, especially if there have been significant changes in legislation or guidance which need reflecting.

STAFF liaison will be usually be planned (CPD, staff meetings) but might be an informal advice chat. It often isn't the time to deliver this that is the issue, it is the time required to develop your presentation!

One way to avoid staff appearing at inopportune moments is to have a 'drop-in' session they can attend, although there will always be someone who is unavailable at the time or has an 'emergency'.

PARENTS have a habit of needing you when you are at your busiest, but most parent meetings can be scheduled. Whilst some parents' meetings can be long, many are quite brief. Remember to write your notes in the meeting. You will forget by later! It can be helpful, although it feels quite rude until you get used to it, to say how long you have got at the start of a meeting. "Hi, I'm really sorry but I'm teaching in 30 minutes, do you think we can cover everything by then, or would we be better to schedule something in the diary?" And stick to it. Another one that worked quite well was, "Hi, can you give me an overview of what you'd like to chat about today, so we can prioritse? We both know we won't get through everything, but if we can agree what we will sort today we will know what we need to discuss next time."

PROFESSIONALS are usually scheduled meetings but do tend to be quite time consuming both in length and preparation/ follow-up. For every hour of work/meeting with a professional I could pretty much predict a further hour of preparation/follow-up was required.

Liaison with other agencies and professionals, fortunately, happens at fixed points throughout the year and even if an EHCP is requested you generally have some warning for these meetings. That is not to say that they take any less time. If you're involved in child protection and safeguarding you will know things may escalate quickly!

You need to make friends at the local authority, but be aware that what they tell you, isn't always correct. It is their interpretation of things and many local authorities have been caught out recently with incorrect advice and practices. However, if you ever need to evidence a child's needs for top-up funding or and EHCP then your local authority will often need to sign off part of the report.

Your headteacher and governors need a regular update on the SEN work in school. This doesn't have to be face to face and may take the form of a report.

Isn't it strange how, perhaps the most important piece of work, keeping SEN records up-to-date, is at the bottom of the list? This is also the most time-consuming administrative task of all.

So, by the time we get to the final sections of the Code of Practice (6.90) we find we have already covered the activities in the above, such as checking on the day to day work being done. When a TA calls in sick they are often not covered, and you may need to shuffle your current support around in order to ensure the needs of your pupils are met. As a secondary SENCO it is helpful not to have a tutor group in order to be able to organise this (you'll be the last to find out!), in a primary school it may be more difficult but you could consider using a TA within your own class to take the register and do a 5-minute brain gym in order to give you this time when required.

If you are the designated person for looked after children this can make life a little easier, but if not be aware that they are scrutinised not only by your own head teacher but also by a virtual headteacher. They will be accounting for every penny that is spent on the child.

Especially in a primary school you will have to monitor many children who 'might' eventually end up on your SEN register. The role here actually falls to the class teachers but you may have to advise them on strategies to try as part of a graduated response.

The school budget is always going to be difficult. Do you actually know how much money you have and what it is being spent on? (I give further advice on this in my book about SEN Finance.)

The vast majority of parents we are able to plan our meetings with. It may be a review of the learning plan, or perhaps a discussion about an EHCP application. Sometimes, usually during crisis, they will appear without warning. You will need to be flexible. You can't always drop the lesson you are teaching so having well-trained TAs is essential. Alternatively, a member of the SLT may pick the parent up for you, but be careful they don't start making agreements/arrangements without consulting you first

This hasn't accounted for the fact that you might actually be involved in additional things. For example, it is not uncommon in a secondary school for the SENDCO to be the person who undertakes the access arrangements and applies for reasonable adjustments. It is increasingly common for schools to undertake some of the basic screening assessments with their own pupils rather than asking their local authority, especially as 'traded' services mean they would be charged for requesting this support. Beyond your normal data analysis, you may be required to analyse and report on your SEN data, both as a general group and also in relation to your interventions. None of these are 5-minute tasks and sometimes can be rather long-winded when it is your first time, or if you only do them once a year. I'm one of the few who will admit I like crunching data, but even so, I can get carried away!

Overseeing the day-to-day operation of the school's SEN policy.

- *Supporting the identification of children with special educational needs.*
- *Co-ordinating provision for children with SEN.*
- *Liaising with parents of children with SEN.*
- *Liaising with other providers, outside agencies, educational psychologists and external agencies.*
- *Ensuring that the school keeps the records of all pupils with SEN up to date.*

Strategies for managing your time:
There are hundreds of books on the market and websites that will tell you how best to handle things and no one way will work for anyone. I can only offer what worked for me. I also suggest a good look at Anita Devi's SEND Leader Planner (an active planner for recording the SEN Year.)

I started each year with a really nice planner/diary. One I won't get bored of. Whilst A4 is the best size for space you are more likely to carry around an A5 one. Choose the format of a planner or diary. I found a page-a-day diary worked well for me in Secondary, whereas a 4-session-a-day planner was better in Primary. Decide on loose or spiral-bound (not hard bound, you can't tuck enough papers into it!)

Enter all your school dates into it first. Holidays, school events, data collection points, parent evenings, staff meetings CPD etc. Are there any really busy weeks? You do not want to use those weeks for anything else.

Now enter all your SEN dates. When do you have annual reviews due? Block some time before and after, for collecting information and following up. Do you have fixed dates for top-up funding requests and panel meetings? Have you got deadlines for examinations concessions, pre-arranged meetings with professionals or some dates already arranged for transition events?

Once you've got all of these in you will see which weeks would be better for organising reviews of your pupils or anything else you want to achieve.

This all links to the next chapter on the SENDCO YEAR.

Doing all the above, won't help if you are a procrastinator or the workload has got too much.

Dealing with Post

When you get post put it all in one place until you have uninterrupted time to open and deal with it. Whilst I used my pigeon hole to keep school related things, all my SEN mail had a home in the front file, top drawer, of a locked filing cabinet. I had one evening a week where I would do this straight after school.

When you open post, bin the envelope and write the received date at the top of each item before looking at it. You will be surprised how many medical letters I've received 3 months after an appointment, or even a year after the pupil has been discharged. The difference between the 'clinic' date and the received date can be quite astounding.

Glance at the contents. Decide if it is: destroy (bin), deposit (file), deal with, delegate or deliver. Repeat until you have 5 piles.

Process the destroy, deposit and deliver ones first. (By deliver I mean the letter is better off in the hands of someone else.)

With the delegate pile give each one a post-it note and add some instructions and pass out at the next available opportunity. (My TAs knew I opened the post on a Tuesday evening and if I had any jobs I'd be likely to pass them out on a Wednesday morning in a briefing.)

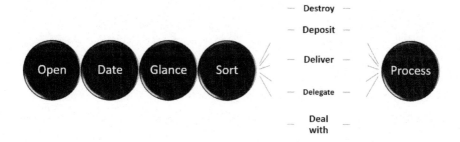

For the deal pile I would already have an idea of what was needed, so it's decision time. Most of the time, dealing with something meant I'd have to refer to other people, so I had to schedule each item into our coinciding 'free time', but if it was simply a matter of sending an email or pulling up a piece of accessible data then I would deal with it there and then.

POST DONE!

Dealing with the Email demon

Emails are an entirely different beast! These creep up on you and accumulate throughout the day. I once went on a course where I had no access to a signal for my phone. I got home that evening to 74 emails – in ONE day. Fortunately, most them were information and not something I had to 'deal' with – but 74!

Sadly, it isn't an option to only deal with these once a week! My first suggestion is to learn how to filter and sort your emails. I love colour coding mine in Outlook and I have filters set to check emails as they come in, apply the colour tag and put them in the right folder for me. Of course, some slip into my unfiltered inbox, but they get dealt with. I particularly like this method as when I was waiting for specific responses I only had one folder to check which was really helpful if I had only a few spare minutes.

Anyway, talk to someone in your school about filtering emails…or play about with the settings and learn by trial and error (ahem!)

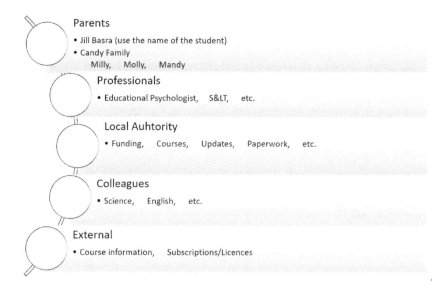

Parents
- Jill Basra (use the name of the student)
- Candy Family
  Milly,   Molly,   Mandy

Professionals
- Educational Psychologist,   S&LT,   etc.

Local Auhtority
- Funding,   Courses,   Updates,   Paperwork,   etc.

Colleagues
- Science,   English,   etc.

External
- Course information,   Subscriptions/Licences

The other useful tip here is to have two school email addresses. One is a staff email address, "as if you are a teacher only," and this is used to communicate with you the same as anyone else in the school – e.g. staff meeting cancelled, arrangements for non-uniform day Friday.

The other address is your senco@ (or similar). This is the address you use for SEN related communications, both internally and externally. It can be a challenge getting staff in your own school to pick the right one sometimes, but if they do it really helps you filter the information.

Once your emails are going to the right places, set aside a time each day to read and respond. You can handle emails the same way as paper mail. Bin what you don't need, forward the ones you can deliver to elsewhere, or delegate (with a note), file (or print and file if necessary) and deal with.

Now that makes it sound like I only checked my emails once a day...who am I trying to kid? I had my emails ping straight to my phone (I still do, big mistake, please do not do this). I would read the header and if I felt I needed to respond immediately/soon then I would. When I was busy I only checked my emails at my chosen time. (For me this was 7:30-8:00 every morning with a cup of tea, the time I arrived at school to avoid the traffic!)

Some days you need more time to deal with the contents of an email and although most only need 5-10 minutes finding that time can be tricky. I used to do a mop-up towards the end of lunch whilst finishing another cup of tea! It worked for me, but if you don't want to give up part of your lunch (no one can make you) then you need to identify an alternative time.

The Post-It© Note Nightmare

Do you know the one I mean? It's where you get back to your desk to find 15 different notes have been left for you to deal with, most of which you need to decipher and none of which have a name on. For me, it was never the worry of dealing with the ones I found on my desk, or shoved under the door, it was the ones that managed to get stuck to the underside of my laptop and only found three weeks later.

I had two strategies for this. The first was to request notes were sent by email. (Actually, we had a messaging system in school which we used, but an email works just as well.)

The second was to leave a note pad and plastic wallet on my desk that was clearly headed 'Messages for Abigail'.

I had to be really firm and make it clear that any messages not left there would not be picked up...and I had to enforce it too.

It may sound really pedantic, but I also had a couple of headers on the notepad and a sticker on the plastic wallet that showed the information I needed. (Blank version available at the back of the book and on the website.)

My gatekeeper, who would pick up phone calls for me, would pop her notes into the same place. She was pretty good at recording things in a helpful manner and almost acted as a role model for the other staff.

None of those helped me to deal with what the messages required me to do, but they did cut down on wasted time trying to find notes or work out who left them.

Blocking Tasks

Try blocking tasks. As boring as it might be to do the same thing continuously for several hours (and not something we recommend for our pupils), if you can possibly bear it try to block repetitive tasks and do them one after another until complete. Recent business research has shown this to be the most effective time-management skill rather than multi-tasking.

One advantage is that you get quicker as you go through, the other is that you generally have all the resources you need to get the job done after the first couple. Examples here include crunching data, writing passports/plans or, my real bug-bear, reading pupil transfer files and extracting their SEN information. As some tasks can be quite untidy this limits the amount of times you need to tidy it all away only to get it out again.

To Do or not To Do

Use a To Do List. It is immensely satisfying to tick (or scribble, scrawl, obliterate...) things off the list. It can also help you to prioritise what needs doing first, especially if things are starting to pile up.

I have a really strange memory for things and I don't usually need a reminder of what I need to do, I already know...I just probably don't want to do what would be on the list! I didn't use a To Do list all the time, just when I had too many things to remember, or when I needed to drop the not-so-subtle hint to leadership that I am already spinning several plates please do not add any more. My To Do lists were more for others than they were for myself.

I am also the ultimate procrastinator and if there was an easier (or more enjoyable) job to do instead of what I should be doing then I would dive straight in! With a To Do list I could chose the order of tasks and 'reward' myself with the ones I liked doing. (It's no different to writing these books – I enjoy the researching and creating blank proforma for you, not so much stringing it all into coherent sentences and certainly not proof-reading! I have to stagger the tasks and reward myself every chapter with 20 minutes reading/research or the chance to produce a new download.)

Tidy

I am NOT a tidy individual. This is not natural for me and I find a tidy desk is too sterile for me to work productively. I am however, organised. I know exactly what is in each pile and whether it is near the top or bottom (and why). I work in organised chaos.

End of paragraph – I can't offer any advice because I know I wouldn't follow it myself!

Gatekeeper

Use a gatekeeper when you really need to get something completed. If you only do this when absolutely necessary others will begin to respect your time far more.

My gatekeeper was the safeguarding and attendance officer. She would sit in my room on a Wednesday evening, provide me with tea and biscuits (do you notice a theme?) and ward off anyone who tried to come in and interrupt. Having an idea of my role, she was often able to take notes if needed or make an informed decision whether it was important enough to interrupt me. The filing cabinets were in my room, so she used the time to do her filing (and mine). One hour of uninterrupted time and we were both able to achieve our goals. Not having any admin support I had my phone calls filtered through her too.

Phone Calls

If you are a class teacher you cannot be called away to constantly take phone calls. Have Reception take messages or put callers through to a Gatekeeper or TA. Specify exactly how you want messages taken. Name, time of call, and a contact number with short message. The most important thing – never let them say that YOU will call them back. This is because we are going to delegate that bit where possible.

Delegate

If someone else has the skills, knowledge, time and access to the information required to do something for you – then let them! They don't have to be big jobs either, taking responsibility for little, but repetitive, things can really free up time for you.

Some examples of delegated tasks...

- ~ Train a TA to collect the information about who receives each intervention and how you want it recording.
- ~ When faced with a staff absence, my team would organise cover between themselves, only referring to me if it wasn't possible to do, or it meant a doubling up of groups/support.
- ~ Completing (and aiding the completion of) paperwork for external services. I was a little more controlling here, they collected the information on a photocopy and I would have the final say about what was sent off.
- ~ One of my team was responsible each day for any unexpected visitors and to take appropriate notes for me to deal with.
- ~ We had a team briefing every morning, but I only led twice a week. On the other days I would be in the room, listening but usually doing something else, and the team would hold the briefing themselves. I was there to chip in and offer advice when needed, sometimes I wanted to deliver a message, but generally, they were able to do what was needed. Although this started off with one designated member of staff to lead the meeting, it gathered momentum to

the point where they had their own routine. Let your staff develop.

~ Have stock letters and just add a paragraph or two of personalised information. This way you can use any admin support to send letters for you.

~ Train your TAs to do objective observations. If I walk into a classroom the pupils behave differently and I'm never going to get a true observation of their behaviour. TAs who they see regularly they tend not to put on a performance for. There is still a place for me to observe, but this process gives me more information to work with.

~ Returning telephone calls to gather more information or book appointments.

The SENDCO Year

There are a great many tasks that the SENDCO has to undertake throughout the academic year. Some are related to the whole school calendar like parents' evenings, whereas others are specific to your role as SENDCO (Annual reviews).

In the chapter on managing time, we considered a diary/planner for blocking our time. But what else do we have to fit into that calendar?

The list below is not exhaustive, nor is it compulsory, but gives you some idea of what you may need to consider, beyond the normal school schedule. In the appendix, I've included an idea of what my year used to look like, but of course, your school is not mine and you will need to move things around to match so a blank version is also included and available at www.sendcosolutions.co.uk or you could use Anita Devi's SEND Leader Planner available from her website https://www.anitadevi.com/ADL-Shop.php.

I present the suggestions as a series of questions at the end of each section:

Financial Tasks

You may have to take responsibility for a number of financial elements and unlike most departments in a school you actually generate money as well as spend it. Generating money comes with its own skill set and a great degree of time. The majority of your money will come from the school budget and an element known as the notional (element 2) SEN budget. If you have pupil premium or LAC responsibility, try to keep your figures separate if possible. There is another element of money (called element 3, or top-up/high needs funding) which is held by your local authority. You are able to put in bids for this money to meet the needs of your most needy students. Most local authorities require several pages of paperwork for this not just about the pupil you need funding for but also the wider picture of your school (so they can check you couldn't fund from elsewhere). Be prepared to spend several hours completing this.

You will also need to ensure your interventions and provisions are costed. Whilst this is not a compulsory part of your role, you will find that provision management is much easier when you take control of all parts for yourself. Fortunately, this is something you could do just once a year, or as you set up each intervention.

You may need to report on any SEN spending for the governors. This will involve reading the reports and explaining the expenditure against outcomes.

When is/are the deadline/s for any Element 3 (Top-up) funding bids?

What is your SEND budget – when will you meet the school business manager or Head Teacher to discuss?

Meetings/Training

There are bound to be some fixed dates in the diary for meetings and training. My local authority was reasonably good at letting us know at the beginning of the year about moderation dates and network meetings, they were not quite so good about letting us know about training opportunities. (For example, one year they changed their funding mechanism and sent out the email with information for a training session about it on the same day as the session.)

The vast majority of these things are only going to happen once each calendar year (such as a personal CPD training session) and they don't tend to need any preparation. However, consider meeting with your SEN governor which is recommended every half term. You don't want to step into that unprepared. The same will apply to any CPD sessions which you have volunteered to deliver, you will need time beforehand to prepare.

Is your Local Authority offering any training updates for funding applications?

Do you have any SEND network meetings or SEND moderation meetings?

When will you meet your SEND Governor?

Who else do you need to schedule meetings with and how frequently?

(Local Authority SEND team, Education Psychologist, Speech & Language Therapist, Physiotherapy, Specialist Nurses, ASD team, Counsellor, CAMHS etc)

What about transition dates?

Have you planned in transition meetings?

Have you booked any CPD sessions for yourself?

Are you involved in SCITT/ NQT/RQT/Induction training?

Do you have any NASENCO face to face sessions, and any related 'time off' for study?

Are you delivering staff CPD? When and don't forget preparation time? How will you follow-up/embed?

Do any staff have CPD courses booked? Who will they feed back to, how?

Provisions and Pupils

One of your core roles was to look after the provisions in place for your pupils. This doesn't just mean checking that they are running, but it also means gathering the information generated and analysing it. (The move from provision mapping to provision management.) Whilst your school data manager (or an IT technician) might inform you that licences are about to expire for a product, can you risk them forgetting?

Something that will eat up your time is meeting with parents and pupils to review the plans and provisions. Whilst you can possibly manage to fit these in during a parents' evening there are a couple of things to consider: Is the space private enough to have a conversation with other parents milling around? Do you honestly have enough time on a parents' evening to do the job justice? What will you do for those who don't attend? And, do you have 3 parents' evenings a year for each pupil? Again, in primary, this is easier to manage with class teachers taking responsibility for the reviews and the SENDCO perhaps only meeting parents for one review. However, parents with a complaint will often state they do not see the SENDCO frequently enough if this is the model adopted.

What licences do you have, are they due to expire?

Who are you reviewing on the register and when?

When will you adapt your provisions?

When will you meet parents/pupils as part of reviews?

When are your Annual Reviews scheduled? Leave time before and after for any write-ups.

Do you have a schedule for gathering parent/pupil views about SEND provision?

Do you have an enhanced provision – what deadlines are associated for reports and bids?

Supporting Staff

My team used to get very frustrated on INSET days. They felt that they were very geared towards teachers and not them. They were not too happy being tasked with display work or housekeeping tasks. I felt very torn. I needed to be part of the teaching input offered by the INSET but I wanted to do something worthwhile with my team. In the end we compromised and sent the teaching assistants on relevant courses (or had in house delivery arranged.) Things such as safeguarding updates, first aid, handling training, a series of visits from a diabetes nurse, educational psychologist, speech and language therapist and school counsellor. This also prevented any absences during the school year in order to update those qualifications.

Teaching staff were able to access drop-in sessions. When I first started the school I offered these weekly, but after a couple of years I dropped to fortnightly. I chose different nights (so departments couldn't claim I always clashed with something they did) and I had an open-door at the lunch-time and for 90 minutes after school on those dates.

Have you planned drop-in sessions?

Are any of your staff going to be absent for planned events (religious, unpaid, maternity)?

Do you/your staff need to update any qualifications/certificates (handling, first aid, medical procedures)?

Do you know you need to recruit – when?

Reports/policies

I will never forget my first year at one particular school. They hadn't updated their policies in a while and I stupidly pointed this out to them. I ended up updating all the policies that are required to be displayed on the website, regardless of whether I had any responsibility for them. It was one of the most brain-draining, nightmares of a task I have ever undertaken. Policy writing is not a ten-minute job and no template is ever going to reflect your school accurately.

Census is such an important part of school and yet very few staff know or understand it. The data on the census is what will drive the future finances of the school. It is so important to provide the correct information. Fortunately, with electronic management information systems (MIS) this should make it easier, but the data produced is only as accurate as the data held in the systems. If you haven't updated your SEN register in the MIS then it won't be accurate on the report!

When will you produce your SEN report for the website/governors?

Do you need to write reports for interventions (like an English, History, PE contribution)?

When are school policies due for update?

When is census- what needs to be amended/checked before then?

Data/assessment

Do not collect data for the sake of collecting data! Wherever you can, make use of someone else's data to achieve your purpose.

That said, collecting a set of scores is one thing, it's the time to sit and do something with them that is more important. If you do not understand the format of what you are looking at, or have been presented with, then you are going to need to learn all about that first before you can understand and write a meaningful report.

Examination concessions used to drive me insane! No matter how early I started them there still seemed to be a mad rush to get them all processed in time. Now, that might be because in my school I had to undertake the assessments, complete the forms as SENDCO and assessor, gather the information, and input into the access arrangements website before informing the pupil/parents and staff what concessions had been granted. I didn't have admin support or an assessor to do any of the elements for me. You need to consider what parts of this task you are responsible for and ensure that you have these scheduled in with plenty of time. If you are booking an external assessor this needs to be done in advance since they do book up very quickly.

When will you collect data – can it line up with whole school data collections?

Are you a part of whole school observation schedules?

When will you analyse the data you collect?

When will you assess intervention information?

When will you update reading/spelling ages (it usually falls to the SENDCO)?

Will you have the data needed for examination access arrangements, or do you need to schedule assessments/book someone to do them?

When do examination access arrangements have to be completed?

When do you need to apply for modified papers?

Others

If there were not enough tasks to keep you occupied from those above, here are a few others that you may need to consider.

I was fortunate enough to be able to access timetables towards the end of the Summer holidays and this meant I could spend the last week of my holiday planning my support timetable for the Autumn term. But it only takes one small thing and you might need to undo several hours work to accommodate an unexpected new arrival, or a member of staff who suddenly leaves!

Are you participating in any awareness weeks?

Are you headed towards recognition awards and their deadlines/reviews?

Each year/term you need to plan your support timetable and interventions.

You will also need time to review files of new starters (those that appear in bulk, and the ones that drift in over the course of the year.)

I have drawn most of this information from my own TES post here (well it's not going to change from the article to writing the book!): https://www.tes.com/sponsored/provisionmap/make-academic-year-your-best-yet-our-guide-perfect-planning-sendcos

Some of these things only need to be done once a year, others may be done more frequently. Some are big jobs that could be staggered (for example, reports can be done by year group.)

OK, that didn't help you manage your time and probably installed a degree of panic if this is your first year, but at least you have a nice diary from the time management chapter and can see where you (might) have the time to do all of those things!

A Crash Course in Law

I am not a lawyer, you are probably not a lawyer and the local authority SEND representative is unlikely to be a lawyer...yet we are all dabbling with a policy that is enshrined in UK law. The Code of Practice is a set of guidelines designed to ensure that you are legally compliant with the Children and Families Act and an EHCP is a legal document which is generated for some pupils. You are required to pay due regard to the contents of the Code.

The Code of Practice[8]

This statutory code contains the legal requirements that you must follow without exception and the statutory guidance that you must follow by law unless there's a good reason not to (let's not go there). It also explains the duties of local authorities, health bodies, schools and colleges to provide for those with special educational needs under part 3 of the Children and Families Act 2014.

The needs of most pupils are going to be met at SEN Support, in other words, without the need for extensive advice or support from external agencies. Sometimes we need that higher level of support and sometimes we need to have a formal document which outlines exactly what that support will be and who will provide it. This is an EHCP (Education, Health and Care Plan).

I may have missed a headline (or two) where schools have been taken to court for not employing a qualified school teacher as their SENDCO (I'm sure they were rapped on the knuckles and told to sort it out, or perhaps

---

[8] https://www.gov.uk/government/publications/send-code-of-practice-0-to-25

they 'named' a **SENDCO** whilst allowing someone unqualified to continue in the role...that wouldn't happen really, would it?) but a quick trawl of the internet shows plenty of local authorities who have been legally challenged over EHCPs and in most cases have lost. Special Needs Jungle[9] tell us 86% of EHCP taken to first tier tribunal by parents are won. In other words, the local authority loses 86% of the time.

Just as an aside, there was some interesting, albeit unvalidated, Twitter chat recently. The cost of a First Tier Tribunal to a local authority is in the region of £70, 000 and it can take 18-36 months to get to this stage. At the last minute the local authority will concede defeat and agree to the plan. Why waste £70, 000? Because it was probably cheaper than providing the young person with the support they needed over that period of time!

Education, Health and Care Plan
The EHCP is a document which sets out the Education, Health and Social Care needs a pupil has and the support that is necessary to meet those needs. The EHCP is a legally binding document. It is binding on not only the Local Authority, but also on Local Health Services (Care Commissioning Groups).

As mentioned back in the first chapter there are also legislative matters with which you must have due regard: The Disability Discrimination Act (DDA) and the Equalities Act.

---

[9] https://specialneedsjungle.com/

Be Aware

There are a couple of places where schools come unstuck and leave themselves open to possible action at a later stage.

Oops I'm late

Not applying in time (or at all) for examination concessions (mostly GCSE/A'level could leave you open to accusation of not meeting your legal duties).

Under the DDA pupils with learning difficulties and disabilities have protected characteristics. You must ensure they have what they are entitled to. That does not mean, however, you should apply concessions simply based on their 'label' if they do not meet the criteria for concessions to be applied. This is where many parents get quite angry and start ranting about their child needing access arrangements, but if your evidence indicates otherwise no amount of ranting is going to change things. Make sure you keep parents and pupils in the loop, so they are not finding this out just before the exams start!

Sometimes you will need to challenge other professionals on this who insist their report entitles a student to a particular concession...if the data doesn't say so, then you have a difficult battle on your hands.

EHCP failures

Not doing what it says in the EHCP is illegal.

Legally the Local Authority must ensure the targets from the EHCP are met and the prescribed actions (provisions) are their responsibility. However, the Local Authority will expect you as the named school to do your part and spend a reasonable amount of your delegated budget in ensuring that you do put things in place. If a TA is off on long term sick, it is your responsibility to ensure that the pupil does not suffer – either by redeploying staff, employing cover or contacting the local authority for advice/support.

Admissions say No

You cannot say 'no' to a pupil admission.

If you have been named as the school in the EHCP you cannot refuse admission to the school. You will have already been consulted prior to the final document being produced and asked whether placement of the pupil will be detrimental to the provision and resources provided for other pupils. If your argument against having the pupil has not stood up to scrutiny at that stage, there's nothing you can do. The EHCP is legally binding and you cannot turn the pupil away or unreasonably delay their start date. (No one is going to argue that you need a couple of days to employ a TA or care worker if all your staff are currently deployed. The Local Authority and the parent are not going to want to set up the pupil to fail. Just be reasonable with timescale.)

Cool off

Sending a pupil home to 'cool off', otherwise known as an unofficial exclusion is illegal.

Quite simply you cannot do this, regardless of whether under the parent's goodwill it seems like a good idea for all parties concerned. An exclusion is an exclusion and must be recorded as such. If a parent has regular calls to collect their child 'early to allow cooling off' this is clear evidence that the support structures of the school are inadequate. A savvy parent may soon be chasing down a full set of their school records and making an application for an EHCP! If a student genuinely needs cooling off time, then you are catering for a need under the definition of the Code of Practice and they should be on your SEN register. You should therefore have a provision in place to accommodate the cooling off away from class. If this is not suitable and the pupil needs to be excluded because they have surpassed all reasonable boundaries then it may be worth considering your provisions and what is triggering the behaviours. If you don't know the responses to this, then an EHCP is needed to find those answers.

Funding fallacies

Falling for the funding myths.

This one is complicated. Schools receive an amount of money per child (the AWPU, average weighted pupil unit, or Element 1 funding) and then an additional amount for each 'SEN' child (called the notional budget, Element 2 funding, and based on EYFS levels in primary schools and KS2 levels for secondary schools.) This funding is not ringfenced (although there are many arguments which say it should be.) It is the notional budget that causes confusion. Whilst the Code of Practice suggests that this money be spent on meeting the needs of pupils at school support, it does not specify that the full amount has to be spent on an 'individual' child in order for them to a) apply for an EHCP, or b) apply for top-up (Element 3, high needs funding). Sadly, this is the interpretation most Local Authorities who will dictate that you must evidence spending this notional £6,000 solely on an individual before they will consider applications under either scenario. This is not a legally sound basis from the Local Authority and you are well within your rights to challenge it – however, I firmly suggest you request support from others and make sure you have the evidence that you are providing the pupil with appropriate levels of support/intervention. You can't apply for element 3 funding just because you've run out of all other money! Sometimes, the Local Authority will dictate a number of hours that a pupil must receive support for before they will consider element 3 funding or an EHCP, again this is not legally sound. Sadly, you might need to ruffle a few feathers and make a few enemies on the course to winning this argument.

Conclusion

Whilst the role of SENDCO is no doubt one of the most rewarding, it is also the one that can be both the most lonely and the most varied!

You will be required to wear many hats as the SENDCO and that's without taking into consideration you may have other roles in school too. As the sole SENDCO in the school (at least in the majority of schools) you will also find yourself constantly thinking on your feet having to make decisions on a daily basis without necessarily having a colleague to advise, support or bounce ideas off.

There is much talk about the 'strategic SENDCO' one who plans and co-ordinates for the pupils identified which is a cold, clinical approach to the work. A SENDCO is more likely to have originally come from the nurturing and caring side of things and be drawn to the role from a desire to assist those pupils who need it the most. Balancing those two things will be one of the toughest challenges you face. Before you can become strategic you need to know your role and know your SEN and hopefully this book has helped with your understanding of the first of these.

Appendices

My SENDCO Year (an excerpt)

SEPTEMBER	School	SENDCO
Week 1	First week, settling in INSET (Mon) – ½ day CPD on Inclusion, Me to deliver	Support timetables Distribute SEN information New staff induction Tues Analyse Summer results data
Week 2	Department Meeting Wed	Annual Review due (TC) Wed Meet new Ed Psy Tues Renew CATs Licences Write admissions policy
Week 3	Staff Meeting Wed (Hand in Y9 Lit books for scrutiny) Non-uniform Fri Y7 team building day Tues – need 3 TAs	Reading tests Y9 Mon Plan CAMHS support Follow-up on Inclusion CPD Drop-in session Thurs Cross-check MIS entries for new starters (SEND)
Week 4	Transition Day Tues (Y5+6) Transition Evening Tues(Y6) Whole school data collection (Y9) and observations/scrutiny	Meet new SEND Governor/Tour Mon Attend governors and present report on Summer results Thurs 2xTA + 3NQT out on Autism awareness training Thurs
OCTOBER		
Week 5	Settling-in evening (Y7) Thurs INSET day (Fri) – ½ TAs First Aid course ½ TAs Safeguarding course Staff CPD: Marking policies (only required for first half)	Element 3 bids due in 3 weeks for Y7 (use other half of INSET day) Drop-in session Tues Visit KB at primary school (Wed) Interviews for TA maternity cover Mon

A Blank SENDCO Year

	School	SENDCO
SEPTEMBER		
OCTOBER		
NOVEMBER		
DECEMBER		
JANUARY		
FEBRUARY		
MARCH		
APRIL		
MAY		
JUNE		
JULY		
AUGUST		

(Create your own version or download the one from the website. Split each month into the relevant number of weeks. Add another one or two columns for Personal and Teaching)

Message Log

Messages for Abigail

Please include the DATE, TIME you left the message, WHO you are and some brief NOTES.

Example messages:

| 01.04.18. | 9:20am. | SM. |

Can you call back the Ed Psy on her mobile before 11:00am, she's meeting TC parents later and needs some background info

| 01.04.18. | 12:15pm. | CH. |

I'm struggling with behaviour of JG since she came back? Any strategies?

| 01.04.18. | 13:40pm. | TA. |

All 6 students scheduled for Lexia did not show. They are not happy about missing PE so voted with their feet. PE allowed them to change and stay for the lesson.

Books/Sites I suggest:

Rita Cheminais: Handbook for Sencos

978-1446274194 Sage Publications

https://uk.sagepub.com/en-gb/eur/home

Anita Devi: SEND Leader Planner

https://www.anitadevi.com/ADL-Shop.php

Special Needs Jungle

https://specialneedsjungle.com/

SEND Code of Practice (0-25) 2015:

https://www.gov.uk/government/publications/send-code-of-practice-0-to-25

About the Author

Abigail Hawkins is the Director at SENDCO Solutions. She works as the in-house SENDCO and DSL consultant with Edukey Education Ltd.

About SENDCO Solutions... Abigail Hawkins was a SENDCO for over 20 years of her teaching career. With experience across the whole age range (from 2 years to adults) and across a wide variety of settings and subjects, she is well placed to provide SEN advice for SENDCOs who have simply run out of ideas/juice! Whether you need a shoulder to cry on, a sympathetic ear, support with processes or paperwork, planning for the future, or fighting the current fire, Abigail can provide the advice and support you need to succeed in your role.

The SENDCO's SENDCO

www.sendcosolutions.co.uk

abigail@sendcosolutions.co.uk

Printed in Great Britain
by Amazon

55388936R00031